TOP 10 BASEBALL SHORTSTOPS

Bill Deane

SPORTS TOP 10

Enslow Publishers, Inc.

40 Industrial Road	PO Box 38
Box 398	Aldershot
Berkeley Heights, NJ 07922	Hants GU12 6BP
USA	UK

http://www.enslow.com

Dedication

To Kim, #1 on the list of Top 10 Pen-Pals.

Acknowledgments

The author wishes to thank Bryan Reilly (PF Sports Images) and Mark Rucker (Transcendental Graphics), for their help in providing the photographs for this book; Scot Mondore, Bruce Markusen, Dan Bennett, and Tim Wiles of the National Baseball Library & Archive, for their research assistance; and Sarah Deane, for her usual expert editorial help.

Library of Congress Cataloging-in-Publication Data

Deane, Bill.
    Top 10 baseball shortstops / Bill Deane.
        p. cm. — (Sports top 10)
    Includes bibliographical references (p. 46) and index.
    Summary: Discusses the baseball careers and private lives of ten of the best shortstops ever to play the game: Luis Aparicio, Luke Appling, Ernie Banks, Lou Boudreau, Joe Cronin, Barry Larkin, Cal Ripken, Ozzie Smith, Arky Vaughan, and Honus Wagner.
    ISBN 0-7660-1128-3
    1. Baseball players—United States—Biography—Juvenile literature.
2. Baseball players—Rating of—United States—Juvenile literature.
3. Shortstop (Baseball)—United States—Juvenile literature. [1. Baseball players.] I. Title. II. Title: Top ten baseball shortstops. III. Series.
GV865.A1D3736 1999
796.357'092'273—dc21
    [B]   98-44951
                                                CIP
                                                AC

Printed in the United States of America

10 9 8 7 6 5 4 3 2 1

To Our Readers:
All Internet addresses in this book were active and appropriate when we went to press. Any comments or suggestions can be sent by e-mail to Comments@enslow.com or to the address on the back cover.

Illustration Credits: PF Sports Images, pp. 7, 10, 14, 19, 22, 27, 29, 30, 33, 35, 37; Transcendental Graphics, pp. 9, 13, 17, 21, 25, 39, 41, 42, 45.

Cover Illustration: PF Sports Images

Cover Description: Cal Ripken, Jr.

Interior Design: Richard Stalzer

CONTENTS

Introduction

WHAT MAKES A GREAT SHORTSTOP? The main ingredient is defense. A shortstop is usually a team's best fielder. He needs a lot of range, to reach balls hit to either side of him. He needs a strong arm, to make the long throws from "deep in the hole." He needs the agility and timing to turn a double play. And he needs the brains and leadership to coordinate the rest of the defensive players.

One of the best statistics to rate shortstops is chances accepted per game, or range factor (RF). Chances accepted include putouts and assists made by a fielder. The more balls a fielder reaches and turns into outs, the higher his RF. A range factor of 4.5 is good, and 5 is outstanding. (Range factors were higher in baseball's early days because there were more ground balls hit.) Another important stat is fielding percentage (PCT): chances accepted divided by total chances (including errors). This helps tell us how sure-handed a fielder is. A PCT of .960 is good, and .975 is excellent. (Percentages were lower in earlier days, because gloves were smaller and fields were not as well maintained.)

Most shortstops are not very good hitters. Teams can afford to carry a weak hitter if he is doing the job at a key defensive position. But a shortstop who contributes on offense as well as defense is a rare treasure. The very best shortstops of all-time could handle a bat as well as a glove.

In selecting the ten best shortstops, we had to leave out several great ones. These include old-time standouts Dave Bancroft and Bobby Wallace, Negro Leagues immortal John "Pop" Lloyd, recent Hall of Fame electee Robin Yount, and up-and-coming stars like Alex Rodriguez, Derek Jeter, Nomar Garciaparra, and Edgar Renteria. But there is no shame in finishing behind the ten we did choose.

CAREER STATISTICS

Player	G	AB	R	H	HR	RBI	SB	AVG	RF	PCT
LUIS APARICIO	2,599	10,230	1,335	2,677	83	791	506	.262	4.87	.972
LUKE APPLING	2,422	8,856	1,319	2,749	45	1,116	179	.310	5.24	.948
ERNIE BANKS	2,528	9,421	1,305	2,583	512	1,636	50	.274	4.91	.969
LOU BOUDREAU	1,646	6,029	861	1,779	68	789	51	.295	5.13	.973
JOE CRONIN	2,124	7,579	1,233	2,285	170	1,424	87	.301	5.18	.952
BARRY LARKIN	1,546	5,708	955	1,713	156	718	315	.300	4.47	.974
CAL RIPKEN, JR.	2,704	10,433	1,510	2,878	384	1,514	36	.276	4.62	.979
OZZIE SMITH	2,573	9,396	1,257	2,460	28	793	580	.262	5.03	.978
ARKY VAUGHAN	1,817	6,622	1,173	2,103	96	926	118	.318	5.24	.951
HONUS WAGNER	2,792	10,430	1,736	3,415	101	1,732	722	.327	5.63	.940

Stats through 1998 season.

G=Games
AB=At-Bats
R=Runs
H=Hits
HR=Home Runs

RBI=Runs Batted In
SB=Stolen Bases
AVG=Batting Average
RF=Range Factor
PCT=Fielding Percentage

LUIS APARICIO

LUIS APARICIO, SR., HAD PLAYED BALL in South and Central America for two decades. He was considered the greatest shortstop in Venezuelan League history. Now, at age forty-one, he knew it was time to retire and pass the torch to a new star shortstop.

On November 18, 1953, Aparicio played his last game for the Maracaibo Gavilanes. After making his first putout, Aparicio ordered the game to be stopped. He called for his nineteen-year-old son, Luis, Jr., to come onto the field. In a touching ceremony, father gave son his glove and his position on the team. The torch had been passed.

Luis Ernesto Aparicio, Jr., was born April 29, 1934, in Maracaibo, Venezuela. He grew up on a farm with five brothers and sisters and attended business school in Maracaibo. Thanks to his father, Luis, Jr., learned baseball at a very young age. Like his father, he soon became such a superb shortstop that many pro teams were interested in signing him.

Aparicio began his minor-league career in 1954. He hired a tutor to help him learn the English language so he would be able to compete and communicate in major-league baseball. Just two years later, he was the shortstop for the Chicago White Sox. "Little Looie" (he was just five-feet nine-inches tall and 160 pounds) led the American League (AL) in stolen bases, putouts, and assists, and was named Rookie of the Year.

By 1959, Aparicio was at the top of the baseball world. At age twenty-five, he was already considered the best shortstop and base runner in the game. Aparicio helped the

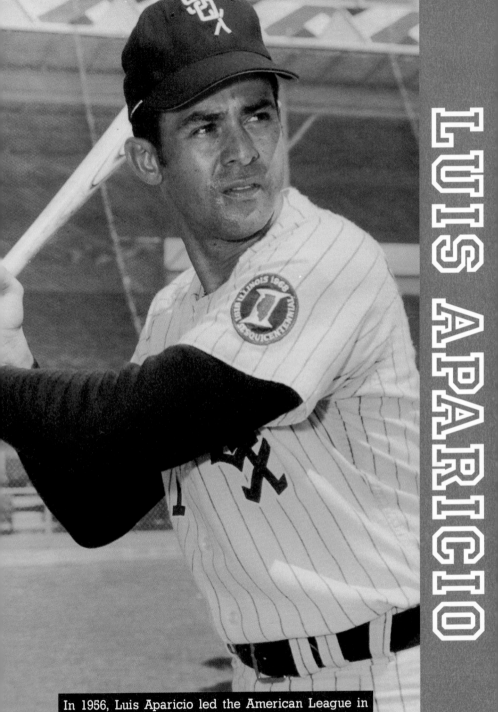

LUIS APARICIO

In 1956, Luis Aparicio led the American League in assists, putouts, and stolen bases. For his efforts, he was voted AL Rookie of the Year.

White Sox to the AL pennant, and he finished second in the MVP voting. That year, a special poll was taken. Each AL manager was asked to name the one man he would choose if he could have any player in the league. All of them named Aparicio!

Aparicio was a phenomenal base stealer. He led the AL in stolen bases in each of his first nine seasons, a major-league record. Three times, he had more than twice as many steals as anyone else in the league. Aparicio stole 506 bases in all and was rarely caught stealing.

Little Looie's greatest asset was his defense. "Aparicio's most spectacular maneuver is on the ball hit into the hole," said one observer. "He backhands it, leaps, twists in midair and throws to first base for a putout or to second for a force-out."[1]

Aparicio led AL shortstops in chances accepted seven times, in assists seven times, and in fielding percentage eight times in a row—all big-league records. A smart field leader, Aparicio won the Gold Glove Award nine times. He retired as the all-time leader in games played, assists, chances accepted, and double plays at short.

Aparicio played eighteen years in the majors, and was named to the All-Star team in ten of them. Although he was not known as a great hitter, Aparicio improved in his later years. In 1970, at age thirty-four, he batted .313, fourth best in the league. He finished his career with 2,677 hits.

Many observers called Aparicio the best shortstop they had ever seen. Among his admirers were Hall of Fame members Al Lopez, Bill Veeck, Phil Rizzuto, Ted Williams, Harmon Killebrew, Brooks Robinson, and Casey Stengel. "I've seen them all," said Stengel, who played and managed in pro ball from 1910 to 1965. "Yet, I've never seen anybody make the plays this little man does. . . . He's the greatest fielder of them all."[2]

LUIS APARICIO

BORN: April 29, 1934, Maracaibo, Venezuela.

HIGH SCHOOL: Lico Baralt High School, Maracaibo, Venezuela.

PRO: Chicago White Sox, 1956–1962, 1968–1970; Baltimore Orioles, 1963–1967; Boston Red Sox, 1971–1973.

RECORDS: Most games at shortstop, 2,581; most putouts (4,548), assists (8,016), chances accepted (12,564), and double plays (1,553) at shortstop, AL.

HONORS: Gold Glove Award, 1958–1962, 1964, 1968, 1970; elected to National Baseball Hall of Fame, 1984.

Avoiding the runner's slide, Aparicio easily turns the double play.

Internet Address

http://www.baseballhalloffame.org/members/hofers/lea/lea.html

LUKE APPLING

Luke Appling is one of the best hitting shortstops of all time. He holds the single-season record for the highest batting average by an AL shortstop.

LUKE APPLING

PEOPLE WONDERED WHETHER LUKE APPLING would be able to return as a major-league star. After winning the 1943 AL batting title, he had served nearly two years in the U.S. Army. Now, Appling was nearly thirty-nine years old.

But return he did. Appling batted .368 during the last month of the 1945 season, then topped .300 in each of the next four seasons as well. It took more than a war to stop Luke Appling!

Lucius Benjamin Appling was born April 2, 1907, in High Point, North Carolina. He grew up in Atlanta, Georgia, where he attended Fulton High School and Oglethorpe University. Appling starred in football, basketball, and track in school, but baseball was his best game. In one game for Oglethorpe, he hit 4 home runs. A scout for the Atlanta Crackers minor-league team was there and signed him on the spot.

Appling played only 104 minor-league games before the Chicago White Sox bought his contract at the end of the 1930 season. He would remain the team's shortstop for most of the next two decades.

After a shaky start, Appling became a fine fielder. He made his share of errors, but his quickness enabled him to reach more balls than most shortstops. Appling led the AL in putouts once, in assists seven times, and in double plays three times. But hitting was what he did best.

Appling had a tremendous talent at making contact with a pitched ball. If a pitch was not quite where he liked it, he would usually foul it off. There are tales of his hitting as many as 23 foul balls in one time at bat! If Appling finally got his pitch, he would often stroke it to right field for a base hit. If not, he would take a base on balls. He wore AL pitchers out for a lifetime on-base percentage of .399.

Between 1933 and 1949, Appling hit above .300 every year he played except one. His best season came in 1936, when he drove in 128 runs and led the AL with an amazing .388 batting average. He was the first shortstop ever to lead the AL in batting. Appling finished second with a .348 average in 1940 before winning his second batting crown in 1943. Twice he finished second in MVP voting.

Appling was moody yet popular, and famous for complaining about his health. It was hard for his opponents to take him too seriously, because Appling played regularly year after year until he was forty-three years old. They nicknamed Appling "Old Aches and Pains."

Appling finally finished his career in 1950, retiring with a .310 lifetime average. If not for the nearly two seasons he missed in World War II, he probably would have reached three thousand hits; as it was, he finished with 2,749. Appling spent the rest of his life scouting, coaching, and managing in professional baseball. In 1964, he was inducted into the Baseball Hall of Fame, and in 1969, he was voted the greatest player in White Sox history.

Combining offense and defense, Luke Appling ranks as one of the best ever at his position. "He was the finest shortstop I ever saw," said longtime pitcher, coach, and manager Eddie Lopat. "In the field, he covered more ground than anyone in the league. As a hitting shortstop, there was no one in his class."[1]

LUKE APPLING

BORN: April 2, 1907, High Point, North Carolina.

DIED: January 3, 1991, Cumming, Georgia.

HIGH SCHOOL: Fulton High School, Atlanta, Georgia.

COLLEGE: Oglethorpe University, Atlanta, Georgia (did not graduate).

PRO: Chicago White Sox, 1930–1943, 1945–1950.

RECORDS: Highest batting average, season, AL shortstop (.388 in 1936).

HONORS: Elected to National Baseball Hall of Fame, 1964.

LUKE APPLING

Appling spent his entire twenty-year career with the Chicago White Sox.

Internet Address

http://www.baseballhalloffame.org/members/hofers/lba/lba.html

ERNIE BANKS

Ernie Banks was the first of only five players who have won back-to-back National League MVP awards.

EXPERTS THOUGHT ERNIE BANKS WAS WASHED UP at age thirty-five. Once a great slugger, the Cubs star had hit just 15 home runs in 1966, and his team had finished in last place. Even his own manager suggested that Banks should retire.

But Ernie Banks proved them all wrong. Over the next three years, he hit 78 home runs and drove in 284 runs—more than all but four other players in the league. He helped the Cubs to their three best seasons since 1946.

Ernest Banks was born in Dallas, Texas, on January 31, 1931, the second of twelve children in a poor southern family. Banks starred in football, basketball, track, swimming, and softball at Booker T. Washington High School in Dallas, Texas. He also played baseball at the local YMCA, where he was noticed by a Negro Leagues scout. At age nineteen, Banks signed with the Kansas City Monarchs for $500 per month.

Ernie Banks continued to play ball while serving in the U.S. Army in Germany. There, he was spotted by a Chicago Cubs scout. After Banks finished his army duties, the Cubs purchased his contract from the Monarchs. Chicago brought him right up to the big leagues at the end of the 1953 season.

Banks was a major-league star right from the start. He weighed only 170 pounds and used a little thirty-one-ounce bat, but he had excellent eyesight and quick wrists. This helped him generate more power than any shortstop before or since. In 1955, his second full season, Banks smashed 44 home runs, including 5 grand slams. This was twice as many homers as any other National League (NL) shortstop had hit before!

In 1958, Banks led the NL in home runs (47), RBI (129), and slugging percentage (.614). The next year, Banks hit 45 homers, led the league with 143 RBI, and became the first NL player to win two straight MVP Awards. As one long-time writer put it, "Ernie Banks of the Cubs has just completed the most fantastic season any shortstop has ever had."[1] Between 1955 and 1960, Banks averaged 41 homers, 116 RBI, and a .294 average each year. In comparison, other NL starting shortstops averaged just 7 homers, 46 RBI, and a .260 average during those seasons!

Banks was also a fine fielder. He led the league in fielding percentage three times and won the Gold Glove Award. In 1959, he set major-league records (now held by Cal Ripken) for fewest errors and highest fielding percentage in a season. Due to knee problems, Banks shifted to first base in 1961 and played the rest of his career there.

The Cubs were a terrible team during most of Banks's career. They lost more games than they won in thirteen of his first fourteen seasons, and Banks never got a chance to play in a World Series. Still, he never lost his cheerfulness or his love for the game. As Banks says, "I like to do everything in my life with a smile on my face and a good thought in my heart."[2]

In 1969, Banks was voted the "Greatest Cub Ever." A year later, he became only the ninth player to reach 500 career home runs. Then in 1977, he was elected to the Baseball Hall of Fame on his very first ballot. He played less than half his career at shortstop, but Ernie Banks ranks as one of the best ever to play that position.

BORN: January 31, 1931, Dallas, Texas.

HIGH SCHOOL: Booker T. Washington High School, Dallas, Texas.

PRO: Chicago Cubs, 1953–1971.

RECORDS: Most home runs, shortstop, season (47 in 1958).

HONORS: NL MVP, 1958–1959; NL Player of the Year, 1958–1959; Gold Glove Award, 1960; elected to National Baseball Hall of Fame, 1977.

Banks was more than just a great hitter. In 1960, he won the Gold Glove Award for his fine fielding.

Internet Address

http://www.baseballhalloffame.org/members/hofers/eb/eb.html

LOU BOUDREAU

THE CLEVELAND INDIANS AND BOSTON RED SOX had finished the 1948 regular season tied for first place. The AL pennant would all come down to a one-game playoff on October 3. All eyes were on Lou Boudreau, the Indians' player-manager. Many people didn't think someone could be a good manager and a good player, too. They thought Boudreau's job depended on the outcome of this game.

Boudreau went out that day and blasted 2 home runs and 2 singles. He made the right moves on the bench, too, leading Cleveland to an 8–3 victory and to the pennant. As one writer put it, "He was the hero of the day, the man who best responded to the dramatic demands of the stirring clutch contest."[1] Boudreau was named the league's Most Valuable Player, and after a World Series win over the Braves, he was now the manager of the world championship team.

Louis Boudreau was born July 17, 1917, in Harvey, Illinois. He grew up in Harvey, starring in basketball in high school. Though his school had no baseball team, Boudreau played amateur baseball and softball in local leagues. He continued playing basketball and baseball at the University of Illinois, graduating with a degree in physical education. Because there was no pro basketball in those days, Boudreau pursued a career in his second-best sport.

Boudreau began his pro baseball career in 1938. After only 175 games in the minors, he was in the big leagues to stay. In his first full season there, Boudreau played in all of Cleveland's games, hit 46 doubles, drove in 101 runs, and batted .295. He also led AL shortstops in assists, double

LOU BOUDREAU

Aside from being a Hall of Fame shortstop, Lou Boudreau also became manager of the Cleveland Indians when he was just twenty-four years old.

plays, and fielding percentage, and was named the major leagues' best rookie.

Boudreau suffered through many physical troubles during his career, including appendicitis, a broken hand, and an eye problem. Because he had broken his right ankle three times, he was not very fast. What Boudreau lacked in speed he made up for in brains and coordination. He knew where to play the hitters, and he had excellent reflexes and sure hands. "He's got the greatest head and fastest hands I ever saw," said teammate Joe Gordon, a star player of the 1940s.[2]

After the 1941 season, the popular Boudreau was named manager of the Indians. At just twenty-four, he became the youngest full-time manager in big-league history. Some thought the pressures of managing would hurt Boudreau's playing performance. He proved them wrong. Boudreau led AL shortstops in putouts four times, in assists twice, in double plays five times, and in percentage eight times—every full year that he played! Despite a strange batting stance, he was also a fine hitter. He topped the AL in doubles three times, and won the 1944 batting title with a .327 average. His best year was the 1948 pennant season, when he batted .355 with 18 homers and 106 RBI, earning the Major League Player of the Year Award.

Boudreau finished his playing career in 1952 with a .295 lifetime average. He continued managing through 1960, then became an announcer for many years. In 1970, he became just the ninth shortstop elected to the Baseball Hall of Fame. Thus, the basketball star from Harvey, Illinois, joined the greatest baseball players in the baseball shrine at Cooperstown, New York.

LOU BOUDREAU

BORN: July 17, 1917, Harvey, Illinois.

HIGH SCHOOL: Harvey High School, Harvey, Illinois.

COLLEGE: University of Illinois at Urbana-Champaign, Urbana, Illinois.

PRO: Cleveland Indians, 1938–1950; Boston Red Sox, 1951–1952.

RECORDS: Most years leading league in fielding percentage, shortstop (8).

HONORS: AL MVP, 1948; Major League Player of the Year, 1948; elected to National Baseball Hall of Fame, 1970.

Leaping to avoid the oncoming player, Lou Boudreau tries to get the second out.

Internet Address

http://www.baseballhalloffame.org/members/hofers/lb/lb.html

JOE CRONIN

Joe Cronin, then with the Boston Red Sox, takes some mighty cuts.

JOE CRONIN WAS THINKING about quitting baseball. He seemed to be a failure as a major-league player. In both 1926 and 1927, he had made the Pirates' team, only to be demoted to the minor leagues. Pittsburgh released the youngster, and he joined the Washington Senators, batting a weak .242 in 1928. "There were some baseball people who said he was the worst looking shortstop then in major league circles," recalled one writer. "Joe did not field too smoothly at the time. His hitting was even worse."[1]

Instead of quitting, Cronin worked hard to improve. He took endless batting practice, ran four to five miles a day, and chopped wood to build his muscles. He grew from a 152-pound slap-hitter into a 180-pound slugger. Within two years, Cronin had transformed from the league's "worst looking shortstop" to its Most Valuable Player. In earning the 1930 MVP Award, he batted .346 with 127 runs scored and 126 RBI, and led AL shortstops in putouts and assists.

Joseph Edward Cronin was born October 12, 1906, in San Francisco, California. There, he learned various sports at school and in his neighborhood. "From the time I was old enough to toddle away from home, I began spending my time at the Excelsior Playground," he recalled. "I all but lived on that playground, and there I learned baseball, soccer, football, basketball, and tennis."[2]

Cronin turned down a college baseball scholarship, choosing to play semipro ball, then began his pro career at age eighteen. After his early disappointments, he became a big-league regular with the Senators in 1929. Cronin soon became not only a fine player, but a popular and respected one. At age twenty-five, he was named the team's player-manager. In 1933, his first year in charge, he became the youngest manager to win a pennant, as Washington became AL champions.

A year later, Cronin was sold to the Red Sox for a quarter million dollars—the most ever paid for a player to that date. By 1936, he was the highest-paid player in the game. Cronin continued to excel in Boston and was named the major leagues' top shortstop seven times in the 1930s. Between 1930 and 1941, despite injuries, Cronin batted .307, hit more doubles than any other big-leaguer, and averaged 104 RBI per season. He led AL shortstops in putouts and assists three times each, and in fielding percentage twice.

Cronin stopped playing regularly in 1942, but he still found ways to help his team. In 1943, he set the AL record by pinchhitting 5 homers. In a doubleheader against the Athletics, Boston was losing game one 4–1 in the seventh inning. With two on base, Cronin came off the bench, and crack! He promptly blasted the ball out of the park to tie the game, leading to a 5–4 Sox victory. In game two, Boston again fell behind, this time 8–4 in the eighth inning. Cronin entered the game and drilled another three-run homer, making the score 8–7 and becoming the first man to hit two pinch-homers in one day. "Joe is the best there is in the clutch," said legendary manager Connie Mack. "I'd rather have Cronin hitting for me than anybody I've ever seen, and that includes [Ty] Cobb."[3]

After he finished playing, Cronin continued in baseball as a manager, general manager, and, eventually, the president of the American League. He was elected to the Baseball Hall of Fame in 1956, and voted baseball's Greatest Living Shortstop in 1969. Cronin considered himself fortunate: "I really have been a lucky man to have lived a life being around baseball, doing things I really loved."[4]

JOE CRONIN

BORN: October 12, 1906, San Francisco, California.

DIED: September 7, 1984, Osterville, Massachusetts.

HIGH SCHOOL: Mission High School and Sacred Heart Catholic College, San Francisco, California.

PRO: Pittsburgh Pirates, 1926–1927; Washington Senators, 1928–1934; Boston Red Sox, 1935–1945.

HONORS: AL MVP, 1930; elected to National Baseball Hall of Fame, 1956.

Cronin was baseball's highest paid player in 1936.

Internet Address

http://www.baseballhalloffame.org/members/hofers/jec/jec.html

BARRY LARKIN

BARRY LARKIN'S CAREER WAS IN JEOPARDY. In a workout before the 1989 All-Star Game, Larkin had torn up the ligament in his right elbow. Except for a few pinch-hitting appearances, Larkin was done playing for the year. Doctors said he came within a centimeter of suffering a career-ending injury and questioned whether he would be able to continue as a star shortstop.

But Larkin returned in 1990 as if he'd never left. He batted .564 in the first nine games of the season, sparking the Reds to a 9–0 start. Neither Larkin nor the team ever looked back. Larkin wound up playing in 158 games, batting .301, topping NL shortstops in assists and double plays, and leading Cincinnati to the World Series championship.

Barry Louis Larkin was born April 28, 1964, in Cincinnati, Ohio. There, he played Little League baseball and starred in three sports at Moeller High School. Larkin went on to the University of Michigan, where he earned two Conference MVP Awards. After representing the United States in the 1984 Olympics, he became the fourth pick in the 1985 free-agent draft. Fourteen months later, Larkin was on his hometown team, the Reds.

Larkin batted just .244 in his first full season in the majors, but boosted it up to .296 in 1988 and .342 in 1989, the year of his elbow injury. Larkin went on to top .300 for five years in a row. "He is already the best-hitting shortstop in the league, and I'm not so sure he isn't better than [Ozzie] Smith now in the field," said former teammate Eric Davis. "I like his quiet determination and his quiet leadership."[1]

After averaging just 7 homers per year in his first five

BARRY LARKIN

Hoping to hit the ball hard, Barry Larkin takes a big swing. Larkin was the 1995 NL MVP Award winner.

seasons, Larkin turned on the power in 1991. Despite missing thirty-nine games, Larkin hit 20 homers, tying a big-league record by slugging 5 in a two-game span. Five years later, he became the first shortstop ever to collect at least 30 homers and 30 stolen bases in the same season.

Larkin also started collecting awards. In 1993, he received the Roberto Clemente Award as the "player who best exemplifies the game of baseball both on and off the field." In 1995, he won the Lou Gehrig Award for community service and athletic achievement. For three straight years, Larkin earned the Gold Glove Award for his excellent fielding.

Larkin's biggest honor came in 1995. After the Reds started the season with a 1–8 record, Larkin gave a speech in the clubhouse. The team was much better than its record, and it was time to prove it. The Reds turned things around, winning nineteen of their next twenty-two games, and going on to capture the division title. Larkin was named the league's MVP, as much for his leadership as for his playing performance (.319 average, 51 stolen bases, Gold Glove). "He's the heart and soul of the club," said Reds broadcaster Marty Brennaman. "He's just like Cal Ripken, Jr. He epitomizes all the good things about this game."[2] Larkin's manager, Davey Johnson, added more praise. "Some guys thrive under pressure," said Johnson. "Barry's one of those guys. Believe me, there isn't a more valuable player in this league."[3]

When Larkin is healthy, there are few players who can help a team in as many ways. Larkin hits for average and power, steals bases, takes away basehits with his glove, and sets an example for his teammates. As one writer put it, "None does more for his club, day in and day out, than the brilliant Cincinnati shortstop."[4]

BARRY LARKIN

BORN: April 28, 1964, Cincinnati, Ohio.

HIGH SCHOOL: Moeller High School, Cincinnati, Ohio.

COLLEGE: University of Michigan, Ann Arbor, Michigan.

PRO: Cincinnati Reds, 1986– .

HONORS: NL MVP, 1995; Gold Glove Award, 1994–1996.

Larkin led all shortstops in putouts in 1994 and 1996.

Internet Address

http://cincinnatireds.com/update/roster/blarkin.html

CAL RIPKEN, JR.

Putting good wood on the ball, Cal Ripken, Jr., looks to see whether he can begin his home run trot.

CAL RIPKEN, JR.

BETWEEN **1925** AND **1939,** the Yankees' Lou Gehrig played in 2,130 consecutive games. Nobody since then had come within a thousand games of matching that streak. People thought the record would last forever. Then came Cal Ripken, Jr. Starting on May 30, 1982, Ripken played in every Orioles game for season after season. He kept playing through injuries and other distractions. By September 6, 1995, he needed just one more game to break the record.

That night, Ripken not only played his 2,131st straight contest, but also helped his team win a close game. In the fourth inning, with 46,272 spectators and millions of TV viewers watching, Ripken lined a home run into the left-field seats. "To me, it means I've been counted on by my teammates to play," said Ripken about the streak. "It's nothing I set out to do. It's a by-product of a desire to play every day."[1]

Calvin Edward Ripken, Jr., was born in Havre de Grace, Maryland on August 24, 1960. Ripken, Jr., grew up around baseball fields. His father, Cal, Sr., was a minor-league player between 1957 and 1964 and continued as an Orioles coach and manager in the minors and majors over the next three decades. Cal, Jr., pitched and played shortstop at Aberdeen High School and was drafted by the Orioles in the second round of the 1978 Free-Agent Draft.

Ripken, Jr., went up the minor-league ladder between 1978 and 1981, excelling at each level. He made the Orioles' team in 1982 and was positioned at third base. Experts thought he was too big and awkward to be a shortstop. Most middle infielders are small and quick, but Ripken was six feet, four inches and 225 pounds—bigger than any other regular shortstop in major-league history. Nevertheless, after manager Earl Weaver switched Ripken to short in July, he went on to become the AL Rookie of the Year.

In 1983, Ripken really blossomed. He led the AL in runs (121), hits (211), and doubles (47), batting .318, and guided Baltimore to the world championship. He was named the AL MVP and *The Sporting News* Player of the Year.

Ripken continued to have one steady season after another. More important, he established that he could play his position. During his career, Ripken led AL shortstops in total chances five times, in double plays six times, in putouts six times, in assists seven times, and in percentage twice. He won the Gold Glove Award twice, and set three major-league records in 1990. That year, Ripken played in 95 straight games without making an error, finished the season with just 3 errors, and compiled a .996 fielding percentage. "I think I've proven to people that I can play shortstop," said Ripken.[2]

Ripken won his second MVP and Player of the Year Awards in 1991, after hitting 34 homers, driving in 114 runs, batting .323, and leading the AL in total bases. Since then, he has continued with one solid season after another. Ripken wound up playing an amazing 2,632 consecutive games, setting many records, including most career homers by a shortstop. Toward the end of his career, Ripken switched back to third base.

Cal Ripken is more than records and statistics, though: He is a great team player and a fine role model for kids. "He's just a special player," says former manager Davey Johnson. "He's in a class all by himself."[3]

CAL RIPKEN, JR.

BORN: August 24, 1960, Havre de Grace, Maryland.

HIGH SCHOOL: Aberdeen High School, Aberdeen, Maryland.

PRO: Baltimore Orioles, 1981– .

RECORDS: Most consecutive games played (2,632), 1982–1998; most home runs, shortstop (345); highest fielding percentage (.996) and fewest errors (3), season, shortstop, 1990; most consecutive errorless games (95) and chances (431), shortstop, 1990.

HONORS: AL Rookie of the Year, 1982; AL MVP, 1983, 1991; AL Player of the Year, 1983, 1991; Gold Glove Award, 1991–1992.

Ready for the play, Cal Ripken, Jr., focuses on the action. Ripken played in 2,632 consecutive games to become baseball's new iron man.

Internet Address

http://ww1.sportsline.com/u/fans/celebrity/ripken/

OZZIE SMITH

MOST PEOPLE AGREED THAT OZZIE SMITH was the best fielding shortstop of all time. Nobody thought much about his hitting, though. In his first four years in the big leagues, Smith batted a weak .231, worst in the majors. "If he could hit .240 or .250, we'd be very happy," said his manager, Whitey Herzog.[1] Smith was sure he could not only improve, but also become a good hitter. "Hitting .300 is one of the goals I haven't achieved," he said. "I don't think any of us wants to be a one-dimensional player."[2]

Smith kept working and improving on his offense and went on a weight program to beef up his muscles. After batting .243 in 1983, he increased to .257, .276, and .280 in the next three years. Then, he put it all together in 1987. He finished the season with career highs in runs (104), hits (182), doubles (40), RBI (75), and walks (89). To top it off, Ozzie Smith—the former weak-hitting shortstop—batted .303!

Osborne Earl Smith was born in Mobile, Alabama, on December 26, 1954. He grew up in a Los Angeles, California, ghetto. As a child, Smith spent hours at a time throwing a ball against the steps of his home and catching it on the rebound. This helped him develop the reflexes and sure hands that made him such a fine shortstop. Smith graduated from Locke High School and went on to college at California Polytechnic State University.

Smith started his pro career in 1977, and was in the majors a year later. In just his tenth game with the San Diego Padres, Smith made one of the greatest fielding plays anyone had ever seen. A ground ball was hit up the middle for an apparent single. Smith ranged over and started to

OZZIE SMITH

Many consider Ozzie Smith to be the best fielding shortstop of all time. From 1980 to 1992, Smith won thirteen straight Gold Gloves.

dive for the ball. Suddenly, the ball took a bad hop toward third base. In midair, Smith reached back with his bare hand and caught the ball. After landing on the ground, Smith sprung to his feet and threw out the startled batter. "He does things I've never seen before," said Robin Yount, another outstanding shortstop. "His ability to dive for a ball, get back up, and get something on his throw is unbelievable."[3] Smith soon picked up the nickname Wizard of Oz.

Smith really came of age in 1980. That year, he set an all-time record with 621 assists in one season. He also won his first of thirteen straight Gold Glove Awards. Smith took great pride in his fielding. "I think of myself as an artist on the field," he once said. "Every game I look for a chance to do something that the fans have never seen before."[4]

Smith was traded to the St. Louis Cardinals in 1982 and proceeded to help them to the world championship. He helped the team to two more World Series in the next five years and was named MVP of the 1985 National League Championship Series.

Smith continued with his great fielding while improving his offensive game. He averaged a solid .274 over his last twelve seasons and finished his career with 2,460 hits and 580 stolen bases. He made the All-Star team fifteen times.

Smith broke most of Luis Aparicio's records and finished his career as the all-time career leader in assists, double plays, and chances accepted by a shortstop. As Herzog (and many other people) said about Smith, "He's the best ever to play the position."[5]

OZZIE SMITH

BORN: December 26, 1954, Mobile, Alabama.

HIGH SCHOOL: Locke High School, Los Angeles, California.

COLLEGE: California Polytechnic State University, San Luis Obispo, California.

PRO: San Diego Padres, 1978–1981; St. Louis Cardinals, 1982–1996.

RECORDS: Most assists, season (621 in 1980) and career (8,375); most double plays, career (1,590); most total chances accepted, career (12,624); most years leading league in assists (8) and total chances accepted (8).

HONORS: Gold Glove Award, 1980–1992.

As Smith's career progressed, he continued to improve his hitting. His career average ended up a respectable .262.

Internet Address
http://www.ozziesmith.com

ARKY VAUGHAN

THE NATIONAL LEAGUE WAS LOSING the 1941 All-Star Game, 2–1, going into the seventh inning. The Pirates' Arky Vaughan came to the plate. Though Vaughan was an excellent hitter, he was not really known for his slugging, having only twice hit more than nine home runs in a season.

But Vaughan turned on the power in this game. He lined a two-run homer into the upper-right-field stands to give the NL a 3–2 lead. An inning later, Vaughan blasted another long two-run shot to the same place, making the score 5–2. Surpassing the performances of such sluggers as Babe Ruth and Lou Gehrig, Vaughan had become the first man to ever hit two home runs in one All-Star Game.

Floyd Ellis Vaughan was born in Clifty, Arkansas, on March 9, 1912. Floyd's family moved to northern California when he was just seven months old. He got the nickname Arky when a schoolmate learned Floyd had been born in Arkansas. Vaughan later took the first name Joseph, when he became a Catholic, but most people still called him by his nickname. Arky starred in three sports at Fullerton High School, and baseball was always his favorite. "He was playing ball when he was old enough to walk," his mother later recalled.[1]

Vaughan started his pro baseball career in 1931. He tore up the Western League, batting .338 and leading the league in runs scored and stolen bases. The next year, he made the Pirates team. When the team's regular shortstop suffered an injury early in the season, Vaughan took over the job. He did not give it up for the next ten years.

Vaughan had excellent speed and amazing bat control,

ARKY VAUGHAN

Not known for his home run swing, Arky Vaughan surprised many when he became the first player to hit two home runs in one All-Star Game.

seldom striking out. Using a powerful swing from a wide, flat-footed stance, Vaughan batted .300 or higher in each of his first ten seasons in the majors. He led the National League three times each in runs, triples, walks, and on-base percentage, and once in stolen bases. His best year came in 1935, when he topped the NL in batting (.385) and slugging (.607) to earn the league's Player of the Year Award. Vaughan was named to the NL All-Star team nine years in a row, and batted .364 lifetime in those games.

There was never any doubt about Vaughan's batting, but there were questions about his fielding. In each of his first two seasons with the Pirates, he led the NL with 46 errors. Then, Pittsburgh coach Honus Wagner—considered the best shortstop of all time—took Vaughan under his wing. The two became roommates when the team traveled, and Wagner taught Vaughan all the finer points of the game. It worked. Vaughan not only continued his outstanding hitting, but also became one of the best shortstops in the league. He led the NL three times each in putouts and assists, and once in fielding percentage.

Vaughan was traded to the Brooklyn Dodgers for four players in 1941. After two fine seasons there, he voluntarily retired at age thirty-one for family reasons. Vaughan returned as a back-up player in 1947, helping the Dodgers to the World Series, then retired for good in 1949. He finished with a .318 lifetime batting average. Among all the shortstops in baseball history, only Wagner had a higher average.

Vaughan was finally elected to the Baseball Hall of Fame in 1985. President Ronald Reagan, who had been a baseball broadcaster in the 1930s, led the praise for Vaughan: "He endeared himself to fans everywhere as a fine-fielding shortstop, a superior base runner, and a batter who hit for power as well as for a high average and with very few strike-outs."[2]

ARKY VAUGHAN

BORN: March 9, 1912, Clifty, Arkansas.

DIED: August 30, 1952, Eagleville, California.

HIGH SCHOOL: Fullerton High School, Fullerton, California.

PRO: Pittsburgh Pirates, 1932–1941; Brooklyn Dodgers, 1942–1943, 1947–1948.

HONORS: NL Player of the Year, 1935; elected to National Baseball Hall of Fame, 1985.

FLOYD VAUGHAN

Vaughan was elected to the National Baseball Hall of Fame in 1985, fifty years after winning the NL Player of the Year award.

Internet Address

http://www.baseballhalloffame.org/members/hofers/jfv/jfv.html

HONUS WAGNER

Honus Wagner was one of the first five people elected to the Hall of Fame.

HONUS WAGNER

WHEN WE THINK OF THE GREATEST BASEBALL PLAYERS, we usually think of outfielders. Historians might select Babe Ruth, Ty Cobb, Ted Williams, Hank Aaron, or Willie Mays as the greatest of all time. Today's fans might choose Barry Bonds or Ken Griffey, Jr., as the best of recent years. It is very rare for a shortstop to enter such a discussion.

In 1936, experts had to choose the best players from the first six decades of major-league baseball history. It was for the National Baseball Hall of Fame's very first elections. Ninety-five different people received votes, but only five received enough to be elected into the Hall. Three superstars received over 95 percent of the vote. Two—Cobb and Ruth—were outfielders. The other, voted one of the three best players of baseball's first sixty years, was a shortstop: Honus Wagner.

John Peter Wagner was born to German-American parents in Mansfield, Pennsylvania on February 24, 1874. Johannes—the German name for John—sounded like "Honus" to the boy's childhood friends. John was known as Honus Wagner from then on. At age twelve, Honus quit school to work with his father in the coal mines. When he wasn't working, he was playing baseball. "Even darkness never fully stopped me," Honus said. "I practiced until I was called to bed."[1]

Wagner played semipro baseball for several years. His older brother, Al "Butts" Wagner, was on a professional team and recommended that they sign up Honus. The younger Wagner turned pro in 1895 and joined the National League's Louisville team two years later.

In 1900, the team folded, with most of its players transferring to Pittsburgh. Thus, Honus Wagner became a member of the Pirates. In his first year with the team, Wagner won the NL batting title with a blistering .381 average. The bowlegged, right-handed Wagner hit .300 or higher in each of his first seventeen major-league seasons, a record.

Wagner played every position but eventually found his home at short. Known as the Flying Dutchman, Wagner was an excellent fielder and base runner. He led the NL in fielding three times and in stolen bases five times. Three times, he stole second, third, and home base in the same inning!

Wagner led the Pirates to NL pennants in 1901, 1902, and 1903 and to the world championship in 1909. Between 1903 and 1909, Wagner won six more batting crowns. In 1911, he won his eighth title, a record surpassed only by Cobb. Wagner was not just a singles hitter, either. Between 1900 and 1909, no other big-league player had more doubles or RBI than Wagner, and only one had more triples. Honus finally retired at age forty-three, then returned to semipro ball.

More than just a great player, Wagner was a great sportsman. He played wherever and whenever he was needed and never complained. It all helps explain why a Honus Wagner baseball card is the most valuable card of all to collectors. One sold in 1996 for more than $640,000!

There might have been a few players who were better hitters than Honus Wagner, or better base runners or fielders. But nobody could do all those things better than Wagner, and nobody was a better team player. "Wagner is the greatest ballplayer of all time," said longtime baseball executive Ed Barrow. "The Flying Dutchman stands alone."[2]

HONUS WAGNER

BORN: February 24, 1874, Mansfield, Pennsylvania.

DIED: December 6, 1955, Carnegie, Pennsylvania.

PRO: Louisville Colonels, 1897–1899; Pittsburgh Pirates, 1900–1917.

RECORDS: Most years leading NL in batting average (8); most triples, NL (252).

HONORS: Elected to National Baseball Hall of Fame, 1936.

Following through on the swing, Honus Wagner shows off his fine hitting form.

Internet Address

http://www.baseballhalloffame.org/members/hofers/hw/hw.html

CHAPTER NOTES

Luis Aparicio
1. Oscar Kahn, "New Names Dot A.L. Glove Team," *The Sporting News*, November 5, 1966, p. 25.
2. *Luis Aparicio Day Souvenir Program*, July 19, 1970, p. 3.

Luke Appling
1. Associated Press, "Appling Dies in Surgery," *Newsday*, January 4, 1991.

Ernie Banks
1. Edgar Munzel, "New First for Banks—Two MV Titles in Row," *The Sporting News*, November 11, 1959, p. 13.
2. Associated Press, "Cubs' Banks Voted into Baseball Hall of Fame," *The State*, Columbia, S.C., January 20, 1977, p. 2-C.

Lou Boudreau
1. Dan Daniel, "MVP Award Seen for Boudreau" October 5, 1948, "Louis Boudreau" biographical file, National Baseball Library & Archive.
2. Hal Lebovitz, "The Boudreau Story," *Cleveland Plain Dealer*, c. August, 1947, p. 6.

Joe Cronin
1. Bob Holbrook, "Cronin Story: Success on Spirit," *The Sporting News*, January 28, 1959, p. 11.
2. Harry T. Brundige, "Friday the Thirteenth, Lucky for Joe Cronin," *The Sporting News*, December 31, 1931, p. 8.
3. Bob Broeg, "None Better in Clutch Than Cronin," *The Sporting News*, August 22, 1970, p. 18.
4. Will McDonough, "Joe Cronin and Jimmy Fund in On-Deck Circle," *Boston Globe*, November 18, 1983, p. 45.

Barry Larkin
1. Hal McCoy, "Larkin Resumes Pursuit of Greatness," *The Sporting News*, April 16, 1990, p. 14.
2. Rod Beaton, "Larkin's Leadership, Not Stats, Puts Him High on MVP List," *USA Today*, September 29, 1995.
3. Lyle Spencer, "Davey Barkin' for Larkin," *New York Post*, October 5, 1995, "Barry L. Larkin" biographical file, National Baseball Library & Archive.
4. Ibid.

Cal Ripken, Jr.
1. Ann Bauleke, "Ripken Says He Merely Has 'Desire to Play,'" *USA Today*, August 2, 1994, "Calvin E. Ripken, Jr." biographical file, National Baseball Library & Archive.

2. Mark Maske, "At Shortstop, Ripken Always Comes Up Big," *Washington Post*, July 15, 1991, "Calvin E. Ripken, Jr." biographical file, National Baseball Library & Archive.

3. David Ginsburg, "Cal No Brooks—Yet," *Albany Times Union*, July 17, 1996, "Calvin E. Ripken, Jr." biographical file, National Baseball Library & Archive.

Ozzie Smith

1. Rick Hummel, "Transplanted Shortstops Putting Down New Roots," *The Sporting News*, March 27, 1982, p. 3.

2. Rick Hummel, "Oz an Early Wiz with Bat, Too," *The Sporting News*, June 16, 1986, p. 24.

3. Jim Brosnan, "The Man with the Million Dollar Glove," *Boys Life*, March 1984, p. 13.

4. Ibid.

5. United Press International, "Cardinals Miss Their Leader," *Albany Times Union*, July 21, 1984, "Osborne E. Smith" biographical file, National Baseball Library & Archive.

Arky Vaughan

1. Chuck Abair, "Angels' Herman Buddy of Late Vaughan," *Fullerton Daily News Tribune*, April 21, 1967, p. C-5.

2. White House press release, March 13, 1985, "Joseph F. Vaughan" biographical file, National Baseball Library & Archive.

Honus Wagner

1. Honus Wagner as told to Les Biederman, "Circling the Bases with the Flying Dutchman," *The Sporting News*, November 22, 1950, p. 13.

2. Ibid., p. 14.

INDEX